The Surname Arrowood

Susan Morris &
Wendy Bosberry-Scott

ISBN: 1540741958
ISBN-13: 978-1540741950

The question of surnames, their origins, distribution and history, lies at the heart of genealogy as well as being fascinating in its own right.

In the 1980s and 1990s, long before many genealogical sources were even indexed, let alone online, our Surname Report service provided expert assessments of the origins, history and distribution of selected British surnames, using the sources available at the time.

Now, with so many more sources available, we believe that these reports retain their value as studies of individual surnames, and so we are gradually making the Debrett Surname Archive available online and in print for the first time. Some modern indexes have been consulted to refresh and update the reports.

Debrett Ancestry Research Ltd, PO Box 379,
Winchester SO23 9YQ
Tel: 01962 841904
Email: info@debrettancestry.co.uk
Website: www.debrettancestry.co.uk

CONTENTS

Overview

The use of surnames in England began in the Norman period, when surnames were not necessarily hereditary but usually a form of description. Some described the individual's trade or profession; others were nicknames; some gave the father's Christian name; others gave the individual's place of residence or origin.

Different surnames might be used in different documents, or more than one surname given in one document. Early descriptions were fairly elaborate and by the thirteenth and fourteenth centuries these were simpler, but still variable, and indeed the instability of surnames continued until well into the seventeenth century.

Although some Normans would already have had hereditary surnames on their arrival in Britain, the passing on of a surname from generation to generation only became customary in Britain gradually during the course of the thirteenth and fourteenth centuries. At the end of this period most of the population apparently had surnames.

Variations in the spelling of a family's surname continue to be found until the present century. Before this, as most people could not read or write, the parish clerk or other official would write down the name as they heard it.

There are four main groups of surnames:

A - Local names, which describe a person by his place of residence or origin.

B - Occupational names, which describe a person by his trade or profession.

C - Surnames of relationship, which refer to the Christian name of the father or other important relative.

D - Nicknames or sobriquets, coined to describe a person in terms of his appearance or character.

Many surnames have uncertain origins, but the name Arrowood clearly falls into Category A. However, as with many names in this category, the question of derivation is not a straightforward one.

Origins and Early Examples

There are two rives in Britain named the Arrow: one rises in East Radnorshire, flowing 25 miles east to the Lugg below Leominster in Herefordshire. The name of this river is British, and is cognate with the Welsh *ariant* (meaning silver). In 958 the name appeared in charters as Erge and in 1456 as Arewe.

Another river Arrow rises in north-east Worcestershire, flowing eleven miles south to the Alne at Alcester in Warwickshire. We consulted Eilert Ekwall's *Oxford Dictionary of English Place-names* (1987), which draws upon a general survey of early and secondary sources including charters, deeds, the Domesday Book and maps, to chart the various early forms of a given place-name and thus explain its meaning. Ekwall judges the Warwickshire river name, which is again a British one, to derive from the word *arva*, whose meaning seems to be 'running water, stream. There was a river Arva in Gaul.

There is also a village and parish of Arrow on the banks of the Warwickshire river, which appeared as Arue in 710 and Arve in the Domesday Book. The village lies as mile south-west of Alcester in the south west of the county, and obviously takes its name from the river.

A township named Arrowe is situated in north-west Cheshire, three miles south-west of Birkenhead, in the parish of Woodchurch. This name has a separate derivation form a word meaning a 'shieling' or grazing-ground. The word is in Old Norse *erg*; in Irish *airghe* and in Gaelic *airidh* and is a common element in place-names in Cumbria, Lancashire, Westmorland and Yorkshire in northern England. The Cheshire township is unusual in using the singular form of the word, most place-names use the plural nominative or dative (*ergum*). It appears in about 1245 as Arwe, in 1312 as Harche. There is also a lake called Arrow Lough in the south-east of County Sligo in Ireland.

No place-name has been identified that takes the form Arrowood. However, a lost place-name Arrow Wood, or a topographical description that never became established as a place-name, is certainly conceivable, and this is one possible derivation for the surname.

The dissimilar forms Arwe and Harche, both early forms of the Cheshire place-name now known as Arrowe, are an indication of the problems faced in determining which forms are variants of which names. The addition of the aspirant 'H' is a fairly common phenomenon in both place-names and surnames, and thus in looking at the surname Arrowood we also need to look at possible variants with the initial letter 'H'.

Arrowood would seem to occur in some instances as Arwood, a logical linguistic progression. The surname Arrowsmith has similarly become shortened to Arsmith in some instances. However, Arwood, with the addition of the aspirant, becomes Harwood, a much more common surname. Again, there are several place-names Harwood in England: Harwood, Lancashire, was written Harewode in the thirteenth century; Great and Little Harwood, in the same county, appeared as Harewuda

(1123) and Harwode (1327). Harwood in Northumberland similarly appeared as Harewuda in about 1155; Harwood Shiel, also in Northumberland, was also Harewode in 1214. Harwood Dale, in North Yorkshire, was Harwod in 1301. It will be seen from these early versions that the modern place-name Harewood is closely related to Harwood. Harewood in Hampshire appeared as Harwode in 1198; Harewood in Hertfordshire was Harewuda in 1138; Harewood in the West Riding of Yorkshire was Harawod in the Domesday Book.

There are three possible derivations of the Harwood and Harewood place-names. *Har* in Old English means grey and Ekwall judges that the Hampshire place-names means 'grey wood'. This may be the meaning of the other instances of the name, but Ekwall also suggests the meaning 'hares wood' as more probable for the Herefordshire and Yorkshire names. Thirdly, for the Yorkshire name only he suggests that the first element may come from the Old English *haer* meaning 'stony ground': the place is situated on a high ridge.

All of these place-names might gave given rise to instances of the surname Harwood, describing people who lived, worked or moved from Harwood or Harewood. However, the situation is complicated still further by the surname Harward (also found as Harvard), which in some instances will have interchanged with Harwood. Harward's derivation is the surname and personal name Hereward, which means 'army guard' (*Hereweard* in Old English).

5

Thus, an examination of the name Arrowood has to take into account not only the variants Arwood and Arward, but also Harwood and Harward. Moreover, while Harwood is relatively common as a surname, Arrowood, Arwood and Arward are rare, and the lack of many examples, particularly for the medieval period, make the distinguishing of one group from another virtually impossible. A seventeenth-century Arward, for example, might have originated as Arrowood, Arwood, Harward or even Harwood; the only means of discovering which was the case, would be to trace the genealogy of a family back as far as possible.

In 1892 W J Hardy and W Page published *A Calendar to the Feet of Fines for London and Middlesex 1189-1485,* in which there are no references to the surname. The Fine was a means of conveying or settling freehold property, from the reign of Richard I up to 1834, when a Statute was passed to abolish the method and set up a simpler way of achieving matters.

M A Lower's *Patronymica Brittanica* (1860) a pioneering and still useful British surname dictionary, has no references to the surname, neither does any other surname study such as the more reliable *Dictionary of English Surnames* (by the late P H Reaney and updated by R M Wilson).

Distribution

In 1890 H B Guppy published his *Homes of Family Names in Great Britain*, still the only published work on surname distribution in Britain as a whole. His work was based on printed genealogies and a survey of county directories for the 1880s, in which he looked especially at the names of farmers, reasoning that they were among the most stable groups in society. He restricted his study to names that appeared in a proportion of 7:10,000 or higher and does not list Arrowood, indicating its rarity as a surname.

Similarly, the *English Surname Series*, which is very incomplete, shows no reference to the surname at all.

In H R Moulton's *Palaeography, Genealogy and Topography*, primarily a sale catalogue printed in 1930 listing historical documents, ancient charters, leases, court rolls *etc.*, there were also no entries for the name Arrowood. Nor does it appear in George F Black's authoritative dictionary of *The Surnames of Scotland*.

Many of the sources available for charting surname distribution through the centuries are necessarily confined to the wealthier sectors of the population: in general, nobody wanted to know the names of the poor but the names of those with money or land were naturally of interest to the authorities. However, one source that covers the whole of the social spectrum is provided by English parish registers, the earliest of which began in 1538 following a mandate that all parish priests should keep a weekly record of all baptisms, marriages and burials that took place in their parish. A survey of a cross section of parish registers for the years 1601 and 1602 was carried out in 1910 by F K and S Hitching; incidences of a particular surname are noted by parish and county, although with no indication of numbers of references. There were no entries for any variant of Arrowood included in this study.

A search of a selection of miscellaneous deeds covering the period 1300 to 1850 (Moulton's Deeds), showed several Harwoods (in Surrey and Devon) and one Harwarde but no Arrowood, Arward or Arwood.

An examination of the indexes to wills proved at the Commissary Court of London during the period 1374-1625 usually produces a few instances of all but the rarest surnames. No instances of Arrowood, Arward or Arwood were found in these indexes, although there were instances of Harwood, Horewode, Herwad, Harward, Harwodd, Harwarde and Harvard. Similarly, an examination of the indexes to wills proved at the London Consistory Court from 1492 to 1547 produced only one William Harreward (executor to Sir Edward Mowton, rector of Panfield, 20 April 1515) and one Harwoode entry.

A useful guide to the distribution of surnames for the sixteenth, seventeenth and eighteenth centuries in England is provided by the indexes to wills proved, and administrations granted, at the Prerogative Court of (the Archbishop of) Canterbury, in London, which had superior jurisdiction over local ecclesiastical courts where wills were proved until 1858. The PCC thus provides a national index, although it is not a completely representative one, as testators whose wills were proved in the PCC were mostly among the wealthier members of society, and a disproportionate number of them were from London or Middlesex.

A search of the online indexes for the years 1384 to 1858 found nothing for the surname Arrowood or Arward, but there was one entry for Arwood:

> 1682   John Arwood, meale chandler of Staines,
> Middlesex

A similar search for Harwood, over the same period, found 360 entries for the name and 89 entries for Harwarde. Arrowood was thus a very rare surname.

For the nineteenth century, H B Guppy's survey has been mentioned above. Another important Victorian source is the *Return of Owners of Land of 1873*, sometimes known as the Modern Domesday Book. This source lists, county by county, every owner of an acre of land or more, with their residence (not necessarily the address of their property) and the acreage of their holding. There was no entry found for the surname Arrowood, Arward or Arwood.

The IGI was consulted for specific counties. This was an index chiefly of baptisms and marriages complied by members of the Church of Jesus Christ of Latter Day Saints, which was neither complete nor wholly accurate, but served as a useful guide to surname distribution. Arwood entries were cross-referenced to Harwood, Erwood, Orwood and Orswodd; Erwood and Orwood would certainly seem to be possible variants. No

Arrowood entries were found for the counties of Lancashire, Yorkshire, Cheshire, Herefordshire, Warwickshire, Hampshire or Northumberland (these being the counties in which the place-names Arrow and Har(e)wood occurred). However, Lancashire and Yorkshire both showed isolated incidences of Arwood (in Ulverston and Huddersfield respectively) in the eighteenth century. Hampshire also showed Arwood entries in Portsea and Portsmouth in the eighteenth century.

The first decennial census return in England, Scotland and Wales was taken in 1801, but personal information was only recorded from 1841 onwards. From 1851, the age, occupation and birthplace is given for each member of the household, and so these records provide invaluable genealogical information as well as a fascinating 'snapshot' of the family in the nineteenth century. The latest return currently open to public inspection is that of 1911 and there are now national indexes to the returns from 1841 onwards, although these are not wholly reliable. Using the indexes, we found the following numbers for Arrowood, Arwood and Arward in England, Scotland and Wales:

> **6 June 1841**
> Arrowood (7); Arwood (39); Arward (7)
>
> **30 March 1851**
> Arrowood (4); Arwood (17)
>
> **7 April 1861**
> Arrowood (1); Arwood (19)

2 April 1871
Arwood (25)

3 April 1881
Arwood (4)

5 April 1891
Arrowood (1); Arwood (59)

31 March 1901
Arrowood (6); Arwood (39); Arward (1)

2 April 1911
Arrowood (7); Arwood (5); Arward (3)

Two entries for Arwood were found in Wales in 1861 and a single instance of Arward was found in Scotland in 1841; all the other entries were from England.

A search of the online indexes for wills proved and administrations granted in England and Wales between 1858 and 1966 found nothing for Arrowood or Arward and only two entries for Arwood:

1877　Janet Grant Arwood, Middlesex
1950　Herbert James Arwood, Surrey

There were over 300 entries for Harwood but none for Harwarde. It would appear, therefore, that Harwood had become the most dominant form of the surname.

Printed Genealogies

An examination of genealogical bibliographies found nothing for Arrowood, Arward or Arwood. A search of Debrett's *People of Today* (online), found no reference to Arrowood, Arward or Arwood.

Heraldry

There is a single coat of arms listed in Burke's *General Armory* granted to the Arrowood/Arwood family of Lancashire:

> Emblazon: Argent three conies azure (another three conies courant).
> Crest: a savage, his club in the right hand resting on the wreath proper

In *General Armory Two* (1973) we found:

> Arwood – Argent three leopards courant azure
> Arwood – Argent three hares courant in pale azure

It is interesting to see the use of hares (as indeed of conies) in these designs, suggesting a link with Harewood and Harwood. Although this of course cannot be taken as true etymological evidence, it suggests at least that in the mind of the herald who designed the arms, Arwood was derived from Harewood.

Summary

The absence of examples of the specific form Arrowood, and moreover the absence of early instances of Arrowood/Arward/Arwood, suggest that, rather than a linguistic shortening form Arrowood to Arwood, the development may have been in the other direction, from Arwood (derived in turn from Harwood) to Arrowood, perhaps in imitation of the much more common Arrowsmith. However, in the absence of more detailed lists of instances, this cannot be conclusively shown to be the case.

Sources Consulted

P H Reaney, *The Origins of English Surnames* (London: Routledge & Kegan Paul, 1967)

P H Reaney & R M Wilson, *A Dictionary of British Surnames* (Oxford: Oxford University Press, 3rd edition, 1995)

P H Reaney, *Dictionary of British Surnames* (London: Routledge & Kegan Paul, 2nd edition, 1976)

P Hanks & F Hodges, *A Dictionary of Surnames* (Oxford University Press, 1988)

M A Lower, *Patronymica Brittanica* (London, 1860)

C W Bardsley, *Dictionary of English and Welsh Surnames* (1901: reprinted, Baltimore: Genealogical Publishing Co, 1967)

C L'Estrange Ewen, *Guide to the Origin of British Surnames* (London: John Gifford, 1938)

H B Guppy, *Homes of Family Names in Great Britain* (London, 1890)

Ernest Weekley, *The Romance of Names* (London: John Murray, 2nd edition, 1917)

Ernest Weekley, *Surnames* (London: John Murray, 1917)

George F Black, *The Surnames of Scotland* (New York Public Library, 1946)

Edward McLysaght, *The Surnames of Ireland* (Dublin: Irish University Press, 1977)

T J & Prys Morgan, *Welsh Surnames* (Cardiff: University of Wales Press, 1985)

F K & S Hitching, *References to English Surnames in 1601* (Walton on Thames: Bernau, 1910)

F K & S Hitching, *References to English Surnames in 1602* (Walton on Thames: Bernau, 1911)

Debrett's People of Today (Debrett's Peerage Limited: London)

The Oxford Dictionary of National Biography (online, 2004–2014)

The Concise Dictionary of National Biography, Part II, 1901–1950, (Oxford, 1961)

Burke's Family Index (London: Burke's Peerage Limited, 1976)

H R Moulton, *Palaeography, Genealogy & Topography* (Sale Catalogue, 1930)

Index to Prerogative Court of Canterbury Wills (The National Archives: online)

G W Marshall, *The Genealogist's Guide* (1903; reprinted, Baltimore: GPC 1973)

J B Whitmore, *A Genealogical Guide* (London, 1953)

Charles Bridge, *An Index to Pedigrees* (London, 1867)

Geoffrey B Barrow, *The Genealogist's Guide* (London: Research Publishing Co, 1977)

Sir Bernard Burke, *The General Armory* (London, 1884)

C R Humphrey-Smith, editor, *Burke's General Armory Volume II,* (Tabard Press, 1973)

The Return of Owners of Land (1873)

Eilert Ekwall, *The Concise Oxford Dictionary of English Place-names* (Oxford: Clarendon Press, 4th edition, 1960)

E G Withycombe, *The Oxford Dictionary of English Christian Names* (Oxford: Clarendon Press, 2nd edition, 1950)

W J Hardy & W Page, *A Calendar to the Feet of Fines for London and Middlesex: Vol 1 Richard I – Richard III (1189–1485)* (London, 1892)

Richard McKinley, *The Surnames of Oxfordshire* (English Surnames Series III: Leopard's Head Press, 1977)

Richard McKinley, *The Surnames of Sussex* (English Surnames Series V: Leopard's Head Press, 1988)

Richard McKinley, *The Surnames of Lancashire* (English Surnames Series IV: Leopard's Head Press, 1981)

Richard McKinley, *Norfolk and Suffolk Surnames in the Middle Ages* (English Surnames Series II: Phillimore, 1975)

George Redmonds, *Yorkshire West Riding* (English Surnames Series I: Phillimore, 1973)

The Norman People (London, 1874)

Debrett's Heraldry (London, 1933)

J P Brooke-Little, revised, *Boutell's Heraldry* (Frederick Warne: London, 1970)

Indexes to 1841–1911 Census Returns of England and Wales (The National Archives/*Ancestry*)

ScotlandsPeople: Indexes to Old Parish Registers, Testaments, Statutory Registers

Indexes to the National Probate Calendars for England and Wales 1858-1966 (*Ancestry*)

www.ingramcontent.com/pod-product-compliance
Lightning Source LLC
Chambersburg PA
CBHW070255290526
45789CB00004B/1855